Sphynx Cats as Pets

A Complete Sphynx Cat Owner Guide

Sphynx Cat Breeding, Where to Buy, Types, Care, Temperament, Cost, Health, Showing, Grooming, Diet and Much More Included!

By Lolly Brown

Foreword

The Sphynx cat is not your typical cat. It doesn't have a thick, soft coat of fur and it isn't content to spend all day lounging in the sun. The Sphynx cat is almost completely hairless and it is one of the most active and extroverted cat breeds in existence. If you are looking for a fun and friendly pet that combines the best qualities of a cat and a dog, the Sphynx cat might be the right pet for you!

If you think that the Sphynx cat might be the right breed for you, take the time to learn as much about these wonderful creatures as you can. In this book you will find a wealth of information about this beautiful breed including general facts about the breed, its history, and practical information for keeping Sphynx cats. By the time you finish this book you will have a thorough understanding of the breed and you will know for sure whether or not the Sphynx cat is for you. If it is, you will be well on your way to becoming the best Sphynx cat owner you can be!

Table of Contents

Introduction

When you picture a cat, you probably imagine a graceful creature with a lush coat of soft fur. While this image may be true for most cats, it is not an accurate description of the Sphynx cat breed. Sphynx cats are a unique breed that, while not completely hairless, has no coat. These cats have soft skin with a light layer of very fine hairs but they have the appearance of being completely bald. This may sound strange for a cat, but if you have the chance to see a Sphynx cat in person you will realize that they have their own brand of majesty.

Not only are Sphynx cats completely unique in terms of their appearance, but they are widely known for being one of the most friendly and extroverted cat breeds. These cats have high energy levels and they are very smart and curious – a Sphynx cat will definitely keep you on your toes! This breed forms very strong attachments with its owner and they love to spend time with family. In fact, many people describe Sphynx cats as being dog-like in terms of their temperament and personality.

If you think that the Sphynx cat might be the right breed for you, take the time to learn as much about these wonderful creatures as you can. The more you know about the Sphynx cat breed, the better you will be able to make an educated decision. If you do decide that a Sphynx cat might be a good match for you, you will find all of the information you need in this book to become the best cat owner you can possibly be.

So, if you are ready to learn more about the Sphynx cat breed simply turn the page and keep reading!

Glossary of Cat Terms

Abundism – Referring to a cat that has markings more prolific than is normal.

Acariasis – A type of mite infection.

ACF – Australian Cat Federation

Affix – A cattery name that follows the cat's registered name; cattery owner, not the breeder of the cat.

Agouti – A type of natural coloring pattern in which individual hairs have bands of light and dark coloring.

Ailurophile – A person who loves cats.

Albino – A type of genetic mutation which results in little to no pigmentation, in the eyes, skin, and coat.

Allbreed – Referring to a show that accepts all breeds or a judge who is qualified to judge all breeds.

Alley Cat – A non-pedigreed cat.

Alter – A desexed cat; a male cat that has been neutered or a female that has been spayed.

Amino Acid – The building blocks of protein; there are 22 types for cats, 11 of which can be synthesized and 11 which must come from the diet (see essential amino acid).

Anestrus – The period between estrus cycles in a female cat.

Any Other Variety (AOV) – A registered cat that doesn't conform to the breed standard.

ASH – American Shorthair, a breed of cat.

Back Cross – A type of breeding in which the offspring is mated back to the parent.

Balance – Referring to the cat's structure; proportional in accordance with the breed standard.

Barring – Describing the tabby's striped markings.

Base Color – The color of the coat.

Bicolor – A cat with patched color and white.

Blaze – A white coloring on the face, usually in the shape of an inverted V.

Bloodline – The pedigree of the cat.

Brindle – A type of coloring, a brownish or tawny coat with streaks of another color.

Castration – The surgical removal of a male cat's testicles.

Cat Show – An event where cats are shown and judged.

Cattery – A registered cat breeder; also, a place where cats may be boarded.

CFA – The Cat Fanciers Association.

Cobby – A compact body type.

Colony – A group of cats living wild outside.

Color Point – A type of coat pattern that is controlled by color point alleles; pigmentation on the tail, legs, face, and ears with an ivory or white coat.

Colostrum – The first milk produced by a lactating female; contains vital nutrients and antibodies.

Conformation – The degree to which a pedigreed cat adheres to the breed standard.

Cross Breed – The offspring produced by mating two distinct breeds.

Dam – The female parent.

Declawing – The surgical removal of the cat's claw and first toe joint.

Developed Breed – A breed that was developed through selective breeding and crossing with established breeds.

Down Hairs – The short, fine hairs closest to the body which keep the cat warm.

DSH – Domestic Shorthair.

Estrus – The reproductive cycle in female cats during which she becomes fertile and receptive to mating.

Fading Kitten Syndrome – Kittens that die within the first two weeks after birth; the cause is generally unknown.

Feral – A wild, untamed cat of domestic descent.

Gestation – Pregnancy; the period during which the fetuses develop in the female's uterus.

Guard Hairs – Coarse, outer hairs on the coat.

Harlequin – A type of coloring in which there are van markings of any color with the addition of small patches of the same color on the legs and body.

Inbreeding – The breeding of related cats within a closed group or breed.

Kibble – Another name for dry cat food.

Lilac – A type of coat color that is pale pinkish-gray.

Line – The pedigree of ancestors; family tree.

Litter – The name given to a group of kittens born at the same time from a single female.

Mask – A type of coloring seen on the face in some breeds.

Matts – Knots or tangles in the cat's fur.

Mittens – White markings on the feet of a cat.

Moggie – Another name for a mixed breed cat.

Mutation – A change in the DNA of a cell.

Mutation Breed – A breed of cat that resulted from a spontaneous mutation; ex: Cornish Rex and Sphynx.

Muzzle – The nose and jaws of an animal.

Natural Breed – A breed that developed without selective breeding or the assistance of humans.

Neutering – Desexing a male cat.

Open Show – A show in which spectators are allowed to view the judging.

Pads – The thick skin on the bottom of the feet.

Particolor – A type of coloration in which there are markings of two or more distinct colors.

Patched – A type of coloration in which there is any solid color, tabby, or tortoiseshell color plus white.

Pedigree – A purebred cat; the cat's papers showing its family history.

Pet Quality – A cat that is not deemed of high enough standard to be shown or bred.

Piebald – A cat with white patches of fur.

Points – Also color points; markings of contrasting color on the face, ears, legs, and tail.

Pricked – Referring to ears that sit upright.

Purebred – A pedigreed cat.

Queen – An intact female cat.

Roman Nose – A type of nose shape with a bump or arch.

Scruff – The loose skin on the back of a cat's neck.

Selective Breeding – A method of modifying or improving a breed by choosing cats with desirable traits.

Senior – A cat that is more than 5 but less than 7 years old.

Sire – The male parent of a cat.

Solid – Also self; a cat with a single coat color.

Spay – Desexing a female cat.

Stud – An intact male cat.

Tabby – A type of coat pattern consisting of a contrasting color over a ground color.

Tom Cat – An intact male cat.

Tortoiseshell – A type of coat pattern consisting of a mosaic of red or cream and another base color.

Tri-Color – A type of coat pattern consisting of three distinct colors in the coat.

Tuxedo – A black and white cat.

Unaltered – A cat that has not been desexed.

Chapter One: Understanding Sphynx Cats

The Sphynx is a unique and wonderful bred of cat but it may not be the right choice for everyone. Before you decide whether or not it might be the right breed for you and your family, you need to learn as much as you can about these animals. In this chapter you will receive an introduction to the Sphynx cat breed including some basic facts and information as well as a history of the breed. This information, in combination with the practical information about keeping Sphynx cats in the next chapter, will help you decide if you should get one of these cats.

Facts About Sphynx Cats

The word "sphynx" probably brings to mind images of ancient Egypt where gods walked the earth. The ancient Egyptians worshipped cats and the Sphynx cat breed is certainly one worthy of admiration. This breed of cat is known for its lack of coat but it is not actually completely hairless. Sphynx cats have a very fine layer of down-like fur on parts of their body and some of them even have a tuft of fur on the tips of their tail. The Sphynx cat's skin itself is very soft, having a texture similar to that of chamois.

Not only does the Sphynx lack the typical cat coat, but it also may not have whiskers like a typical cat. Some Sphynx cats do have whiskers, though they are usually shorter or fewer in number than usual. Despite the fact that these cats do not have fur, they come in a wide variety of colors. The skin of the Sphynx cat may be any kind of solid or pattern including pointed colorations, tabby markings, tortoiseshell markings, or anything else you can imagine. They also come in a variety of colors including black, white, red, chocolate, lavender, and many more.

Another distinguishing characteristic that Sphynx cats have is wrinkled skin – it is particularly wrinkled around the head and neck. Sphynx cats have very large lemon-shaped eyes and large, broad ears that are pointed at the tip. Their overall size is usually between 6 and 12 pounds (2.7 to 5.4 kg) which is about average for a housecat.

Though the Sphynx cat might look strange, these cats have a number of redeeming qualities. Sphynx cats are one of the friendliest and most social breeds of cat – they love to cuddle with their owners and they are always seeking attention. Sphynx cats are very energetic and they love to play – they can even make friends with dogs and other household pets. If you work a full-time job or spend a lot of time away from home you would be wise to get another Sphynx cat or to give your cat some other form of companionship, be it human or animal.

Sphynx cats are sensitive to cold due to their lack of fur and they have a very fast metabolism that produce enough heat to make up for it. Like all cats, the Sphynx's skin produces natural oils but because the cat doesn't have fur to absorb the extra oil the Sphynx needs to be bathed several times a month to prevent buildup. In this way the Sphynx is a little more high-maintenance than the average housecat, even though he doesn't have an actual coat that needs to be groomed.

In terms of health and wellness, the Sphynx is generally a healthy breed and it has an average lifespan between 8 and 14 years. The range for the Sphynx cat's lifespan is so wide because there are a few hereditary conditions to which the breed is prone – this is also why responsible breeding is absolutely essential for this breed. Some of the conditions to which the Sphynx breed is prone include a skin condition called urticaria pigmentosa, a genetic condition called hypertrophic cardiomyopathy, and a heart problem called mitral valve dysplasia.

Summary of Sphynx Cat Facts

Pedigree: result of natural genetic mutation in a domestic cat with a regular coat

Breed Size: normal

Weight: average 6 to 12 pounds

Body Type: medium-boned, well-muscled

Coat Length: very short where present, peach-like fuzz

Skin Texture: wrinkled but soft, similar to chamois

Color: wide variety of colors and patterns

Eyes: eyes are large and lemon-shaped, slanting up at the corners

Ears: very large (2 to 3 inches tall), wide at the base

Tail: long, whip-like; sometimes has a tuft of hair on the tip

Temperament: very friendly and social, lively and active, devoted and loyal

Strangers: makes friends very quickly

Children: very good with children

Other Pets: gets along with dogs and most other pets

Exercise Needs:

Health Conditions: generally healthy but prone to some hereditary conditions; cutaneous mastocytosis, hereditary myopathy, hypertrophic cardiomyopathy, mitral valve dysplasia, periodontal disease, respiratory infection, skin problems, and urticaria pigmentosa.

Lifespan: wide range, average 8 to 14 years

Sphynx Cat Breed History

Though the name of this breed brings to mind the culture of ancient Egypt, the Sphynx cat is actually a very new breed, having only been developed in the 1960s. The Sphynx was not the first hairless breed of cat. The cat that is commonly identified as the foundation of the breed was born in 1975 to a normal-coated farm cat in Minnesota whose name was Jezabelle. The kitten was named Epidermis and he was joined the following year by a second hairless kitten named Dermis. Both of these kittens were sold to an Oregon breeder by the name of Kim Mueske who used them to develop the Sphynx breed.

At roughly the same time, a Siamese breeder in Ontario named Shirley Smith found three hairless kittens in her home town and she sent two of them to Dr. Hugo Hernandez in the Netherlands for study. Dr. Hernandez bred the two kittens (who had been named Punkie and Paloma) to a white Devon Rex named Curare van Jetrophin and their progeny, along with the kittens bred by Kim Mueske, became the foundation of what is known as the modern Sphynx cat breed.

Chapter Two: Things to Know Before Getting a Sphynx Cat

Now that you know a little bit more about what the Sphynx cat looks like and where it comes from you might be curious to know more about what it is like to own a Sphynx. These cats are very active and energetic, but they are also incredibly social and they love to spend time with their owners. In this chapter you will receive some practical information about keeping Sphynx cats including licensing requirements, associated costs, and pros and cons for the breed to consider before buying one.

Do You Need a License?

Before you bring home a new pet you should always check with your local regulations to see if there are any restrictions. Licensing requirements for pets are different in different countries, regions, and states so do not assume you know the rules. In the United States there are no federal requirements for licensing either cats or dogs – these rules are regulated at the state level. While it is true that most states do not have a mandatory requirement for people to license their cats, it is always a good idea to do so.

When you license your cat you will be giving your cat a number that can then be linked to your contact information. If your cat gets lost and someone finds him, his license can be used to track you down and to reunite you with your pet. Of course, this information will only be available if your cat wears a collar with an ID tag. If you don't want to put a collar on your cat a good alternative is to have him microchipped. A microchip serves the same function but they can be embedded under your cat's skin so he can't lose it. The procedure for having your cat microchipped is very quick and painless.

In the United Kingdom, licensing requirements for pets are a little different than they are in the United States. There are no overarching licensing requirements for cats in the U.K. but you will need to get a special permit if you plan to travel with your cat into or out of the country. Your cat may also be subject to a quarantine period to make sure he isn't carrying a disease like rabies – rabies has been eradicated from the U.K. through safety measures like these so it is important to maintain them.

Do Sphynx Cats Get Along with Other Pets?

Many Sphynx cat owners say that their cats exhibit a number of dog-like qualities. Sphynx cats have been known to wag their tails when they are excited and they love to spend time cuddling with their owners. Perhaps because of their similarity, Sphynx cats tend to get along well with dogs as long as the dog doesn't have a propensity for chasing them. Sphynx cats can also get along well with other pets as long as they are raised together. As is true for all cats, however, supervision is recommended.

How Many Sphynx Cats Should You Keep?

As it has already been stated, the Sphynx cat is a very social breed so it needs a lot of daily human interaction and attention from his owners. If you work a full-time job or if you spend a lot of time away from home, you may need to look into getting a companion for your Sphynx. Two or more Sphynx cats will get along very well but these cats can also become friends with dogs and other household pets. Before you get a second Sphynx, however, you should make sure that you can provide for the needs of both cats.

How Much Does it Cost to Keep a Sphynx Cat?

Many people underestimate the cost of keeping a pet because they only think about the initial cost to purchase their cat. In reality, you need to cover a number of recurring expenses for food and treats, veterinary care, and other costs which can add up quickly. Before you bring home a Sphynx cat you should be sure that you can provide for his needs financially. In this section you will receive an overview of the initial costs and monthly costs for keeping a Sphynx cat so you can determine whether you are able to provide for such a cat or not.

Initial Costs

The initial costs for keeping a Sphynx cat include those costs that you must cover before you can bring your cat home. Some of the initial costs you will need to cover include your cat's bed, food/water bowls, toys and accessories, microchipping, initial vaccinations, spay/neuter surgery and supplies for grooming and nail clipping – it also includes the cost of the cat itself. <u>You will find an overview of each of these costs as well as an estimate for each below:</u>

Purchase Price – The cost to purchase a Sphynx cat can vary greatly depending where you buy him. You can adopt a rescue cat for as little as $50 (£45) sometimes but purchasing a kitten, especially a purebred kitten from a responsible breeder, could be much more costly. The cost of a show-quality Sphynx cat or one with a unique color could be as much as $2,000 (£1,800) or more. For a pet-quality kitten of good breeding, however, the average cost is between $800 and $1,500 (£720 - £1,350).

Bed – Because the Sphynx is a normal-sized cat you will not need a very large bed. The average cost for a small cat bed is about $30 (£19.50) in most cases.

Food/Water Bowls – In addition to providing your Sphynx cat with a bed to sleep in, you should also make sure he has a set of high-quality food and water bowls. The best materials for these is stainless steel because it is easy to clean and doesn't harbor bacteria – ceramic is another good option. The average cost for a quality set of stainless steel bowls is about $20 (£18).

Toys – Giving your Sphynx cat plenty of toys to play with will help to keep him from getting into trouble when he is home alone – they can also be used to provide mental stimulation and enrichment. To start out, plan to buy an assortment of toys for your cat until you learn what kind he prefers. You may want to budget a cost of $50 (£45) for toys just to be sure you have enough.

Microchipping – In the United States and United Kingdom there are no federal or state requirements saying that you have to have your cat microchipped, but it is a very good idea. Your Sphynx could slip outside through an open door or window without you noticing. If someone finds him without identification, they can take him to a shelter to have his microchip scanned. A microchip is something that is implanted under your cat's skin and it carries a number that is linked to your contact information. The procedure takes just a few minutes to perform and it only costs about $30 (£19.50) in most cases.

Initial Vaccinations – During your kitten's first year of life, he will require a number of different vaccinations. If you purchase your kitten from a reputable breeder, he might already have had a few but you'll still need more over the next few months as well as booster shots each year. You should budget about $50 (£32.50) for initial vaccinations just to be prepared.

Spay/Neuter Surgery – If you don't plan to breed your Sphynx you should have him or her neutered or spayed before 6 months of age. The cost for this surgery will vary depending where you go and on the sex of your cat. If you go to a traditional veterinary surgeon, the cost for spay/neuter surgery could be very high but you can save money by going to a veterinary clinic. The average cost for neuter surgery is $50 to $100 (£32.50 - £65) and spay surgery costs about $100 to $200 (£65 - £130).

Supplies/Accessories – In addition to purchasing your Sphynx's bed and food/water bowls, you should also purchase some basic grooming supplies like nail clippers and mild, pet-safe shampoo. You might also want a collar with an ID tag. The cost for these items will vary depending on the quality, but you should budget about $100 (£32.50) for these extra costs.

Initial Costs for Sphynx Cats		
Cost	**One Cat**	**Two Cats**
Purchase Price	$50 - $2,000 (£45 - £1,800)	$100 - $4,000 (£90 - £3,600)
Cat Bed	$30 (£19.50)	$60 (£39)
Food/Water Bowl	$20 (£18)	$40 (£36)
Toys	$50 (£45)	$100 (£90)
Microchipping	$30 (£19.50)	$60 (£39)
Vaccinations	$50 (£32.50)	$100 (£65)
Spay/Neuter	$50 to $200 (£32.50 - £130)	$100 to $400 (£65 - £260)
Accessories	$100 (£90)	$100 (£90)
Total	$380 to $2,480 (£342 – £2,232)	$660 to $4,560 (£594 – £4,104)

*Costs may vary depending on location
**U.K. prices based on an estimated exchange of $1 = £0.90

Monthly Costs

The monthly costs for keeping a Sphynx cat as a pet include those costs which recur on a monthly basis. The most important monthly cost for keeping a cat is, of course, food. In addition to food, however, you'll also need to think about things like your annual license renewal, toy replacements, and veterinary exams. <u>You will find an overview of each of these costs as well as an estimate for each cost below</u>:

Food and Treats – Feeding your Sphynx cat a healthy diet is very important for his health and wellness. A high-quality diet for cats is not cheap and Sphynx cats need more food than other cats to maintain their fast metabolisms. You should be prepared to spend around $35 (£31.50) on a large bag of high-quality cat food which will last you about a month. You should also include a monthly budget of about $10 (£6.50) for treats.

License Renewal – The cost to license your Sphynx cat will generally be about $25 (£16.25) and you can renew the license for the same price each year. License renewal cost divided over 12 months is about $2 (£1.30) per month.

Veterinary Exams – In order to keep your cat healthy you should take him to the veterinarian about every six months after he passes kittenhood. You might have to take him more often for the first 12 months to make sure he gets his vaccines on time. The average cost for a vet visit is about $40 (£26) so, if you have two visits per year, it averages to about $7 (£4.55) per month.

Other Costs – In addition to the monthly costs for your cat's food, license renewal, and vet visits there are also some other cost you might have to pay occasionally. These costs might include things like replacements for worn-out toys and cleaning products. You should budget about $15 (£9.75) per month for extra costs.

Monthly Costs for Sphynx Cats		
Cost	**One Cat**	**Two Cats**
Food and Treats	$45 (£40.50)	$90 (£81)
License Renewal	$2 (£1.30)	$4 (£3.60)
Veterinary Exams	$7 (£4.55)	$14 (£12.60)
Other Costs	$15 (£9.75)	$30 (£19.50)
Total	$99 (£89)	$198 (£178)

*Costs may vary depending on location
**U.K. prices based on an estimated exchange of $1 = £0.90

What are the Pros and Cons of Sphynx Cats?

The Sphynx is a unique and wonderful breed of cat but that doesn't mean that they are the best choice for everyone. Like all pets, Sphynx cats have a list of pros and cons that you need to consider before you get one. In this section you will find a list of both to consider when you are thinking about getting a Sphynx cat either for yourself or for your family.

Pros for the Sphynx Cat Breed

- Very friendly and social breed that generally gets along with everyone he meets.
- Size is average for a housecat – no special accommodations are necessary.
- Fine, short coat does not require grooming – also very good for allergy sufferers.
- Loves to cuddle and spend time with owners, forms very close bonds with family.
- Generally gets along well with dogs and other household pets including other cats.
- Very unique appearance in terms of hairlessness and colored skin but also beautiful.

Cons for the Sphynx Cat Breed

- Skin requires extra care and frequent bathing to keep oil under control.
- Very sensitive to cold and should not be exposed to sunlight for prolonged periods.
- Needs to be fed more often than other cats to support his fast metabolism and high energy needs.
- Requires a great deal of daily interaction and attention – cannot be left alone for long periods of time.
- Not a particularly common breed, can sometimes be expensive to purchase.

Chapter Three: Purchasing Your Sphynx Cat

By now you should have a more thorough understanding of the Sphynx cat breed and a pretty good idea what it will be like to be a cat owner. If you still think that the Sphynx is the perfect pet for you, your next step is to find out where to get a kitten. In this chapter you will receive some basic tips for finding a Sphynx breeder and for choosing one that is reputable and trustworthy. You will also receive tips for picking out a kitten that is healthy and well-bred. Finally, you will receive tips for kitten-proofing your home to get ready for your Sphynx.

Where Can You Buy Sphynx Cats?

If you have decided that the Sphynx cat is the right breed for you and your family, you need to start thinking about where you are going to get one. The Sphynx cat breed is not exactly rare, but it is not common either so you should be prepared to look around a bit before you find one. Be careful about purchasing kittens from pet stores because you do not know where they came from – they could come from a quality breeder but it is more likely they came from a hobby breeder or an unlicensed breeding facility that puts profits over the welfare of the animals.

In the United States, you can perform an online search for Sphynx cat breeders or you can check the Cat Fanciers' Association (CFA) website for an index of breeders. In the United Kingdom and in other parts of Europe, The International Cat Association (TICA) provides a list of breeders for each of its registered cat breeds. You can also try the Sphynx Cat Association which provides a list of breeders as well.

If you don't particularly care about bringing home a Sphynx kitten, or if you want to do your part in reducing the unwanted pet population, you might want to think about adopting a cat. There are many benefits for adopting Sphynx cats besides the fact that you could literally be saving a life by taking a rescue cat into your home. Many rescue cats have already been litter trained and they are often past the kitten phase as well which means that you may not have to deal with typical kitten behaviors like scratching. Rescue cats that are adults are also fully grown and developed so you can get a good feel for their personality – kittens can change in terms of their personality as they mature so you never really know what you might end up with.

If you are thinking about adopting a Sphynx cat, consider one of these breed-specific rescues:

United States Rescues:

Specialty Purebred Cat Rescue.
<http://www.purebredcatrescue.org/sphynx-rex>

SOAR: Sphynx Open Arms Rescue.
<http://www.sphynxrescue.org/>

Bald & Bully Sphynx & Pitbull Rescue.
<http://www.baldandbully.com/>

Sphynx Lair – Sphynx Cat Rescue & Adoption.
<http://sphynxlair.com/community/forums/sphynx-cat-rescue-adoption.24/>

United Kingdom Rescues:

There are no dedicated Sphynx rescues in the United Kingdom but you may be able to find Sphynx cats in need of homes using the following resources:

Stoney Hill Sphynx. <http://www.sphynx-stoneyhill.co.uk/>

The Sphynx Cat Club. <http://www.sphynxcatclub.co.uk/>

The International Cat Association. <http://www.tica.org/find-a-breeder/item/423>

How to Choose a Reputable Sphynx Cat Breeder

The Sphynx cat is unfortunately a breed prone to several inherited health problems so it is extremely important that you get your kitten from a reputable breeder. A reputable breeder will DNA-test his breeding stock to prevent passing these diseases on – he will also take other steps to ensure that his kittens are healthy and well-bred. In order to find a good Sphynx breeder, however, you may have to do a little bit of footwork. Start by asking your local vet clinic or fellow cat owners for recommendations – if that doesn't work, a simple internet search should yield some results that you can go through.

Once you've compiled a list of several Sphynx breeders you then need to go through them to choose the best option. You don't want to run the risk of purchasing a kitten from a hobby breeder or from someone who doesn't follow responsible breeding practices. If you aren't careful about where you get your Sphynx kitten you could end up with a kitten that is already sick. Once you have your list of breeders on hand you can go through them one-by-one to narrow down your options.

Go through the following steps to weed out low-quality breeders and to choose the best option:

- Visit the website for each breeder on your list (if they have one) and look for key information about the breeder's history and experience.
    o Check for club registrations and a license, if applicable.
    o If the website doesn't provide any information about the facilities or the breeder you are best just moving on.
- After ruling out some of the breeders, contact the remaining breeders on your list by phone
    o Ask the breeder questions about his experience with breeding dogs in general and about the Sphynx cat breed in particular.

- o Ask for information about the breeding stock including registration numbers and health information.
- o Expect a reputable breeder to ask you questions about yourself as well – a responsible breeder wants to make sure that his kittens go to good homes.
- Schedule an appointment to visit the facilities for the remaining breeders on your list after you've weeded a few more of them out.
  - o Ask for a tour of the facilities, including the place where the breeding stock is kept as well as the facilities housing the kittens.
  - o If things look unorganized or unclean, do not purchase from the breeder.
  - o Make sure the breeding stock is in good condition and that the kittens are all healthy-looking and active.
- Narrow down your list to a final few options and then interact with the kittens to make your decision.
  - o Make sure the breeder provides some kind of health guarantee and ask about any vaccinations the kittens may already have.
- Put down a deposit, if needed, to reserve a kitten if they aren't ready to come home yet.

Tips for Selecting a Healthy Sphynx Kitten

Once you have gone through the process of selecting a reputable Sphynx cat breeder, your next step is the fun part – actually selecting your kitten! Just as important as choosing the right breeder, however, is choosing the right kitten so do not rush this process! You need to make sure that the kitten you bring home is in good health but you also want to make sure that it is a good fit for you and your family in terms of its temperament and personality. <u>Follow the steps below to pick out your Sphynx kitten</u>:

- Ask the breeder to give you a tour of the facilities, especially where the kittens are kept.
  - o Make sure the facilities where the kittens are housed is clean and sanitary – if there is evidence of diarrhea, do not purchase one of the kittens because they may already be sick.
- Take a few minutes to observe the litter as a whole, watching how the kittens interact with each other.
  - o The kittens should be active and playful, interacting with each other in a healthy way.
  - o Avoid kittens that appear to be lethargic and those that have difficulty moving – they could be sick.
- Approach the litter and watch how the kittens react to you when you do.

- o If the kittens appear frightened they may not be properly socialized and you do not want a kitten like that.
- o The kittens may be somewhat cautious, but they should be curious and interested in you.
- Let the kittens approach you and give them time to sniff and explore you before you interact with them.
  - o Pet the kittens and encourage them to play with a toy, taking the opportunity to observe their personalities.
  - o Single out any of the kittens that you think might be a good fit and spend a little time with them.
- Pick up the kitten and hold him to see how he responds to human contact.
  - o The kitten might squirm a little but it shouldn't be frightened of you and it should enjoy being pet.
- Examine the kitten's body for signs of any illness and potential injury
  - o The kitten should have clear, bright eyes with no discharge.
  - o The ears should be clean and clear with no discharge or inflammation.
  - o The kitten's stomach may be round but it shouldn't be distended or swollen.

- o The kitten should be able to walk and run normally without any mobility problems.
- Narrow down your options and choose the kitten that you think is the best fit.

Once you've chosen your Sphynx kitten, ask the breeder about the next steps. Do not take the kitten home if it isn't at least 8 weeks old and unless it has been fully weaned and eating solid food. Any reputable breeder will not try to sell you a kitten that isn't already weaned or at least 8 weeks old.

Preparing Your Home

You have probably heard the saying that "curiosity killed the cat" and that is the last thing you want to happen to your Sphynx. You cannot stop your cat from being a little mischievous, but you can limit the number of potentially dangerous things he can get into. <u>Preparing your home by kitten-proofing it is very important but also fairly easy to do – just follow these steps</u>:

- Place all food in lidded containers or keep it in the pantry – you don't want your cat getting into something that could be bad for him.

- Remove any poisonous plants from your home or put them somewhere your cat can't reach them.

- Lock up all of your cleaning supplies and other household chemicals in a cupboard or cabinet.

- Make sure you don't leave any medications or toiletries out on the counter where you cat could get into them.

- Always unplug electrical cords when they aren't in use and wrap them up so your cat isn't tempted to play with the dangling cord – this is a good idea for blind cords as well.

- Keep the lid on your toilet seat down so your cat isn't tempted to drink from it – it will also keep a small kitten from accidentally falling in.

- Make sure that your window screens are very secure, especially if your cat is able to jump up into the window.

- Always check doorways and appliance doors (like the dryer) before closing them – you never know when your kitten might climb in.

Chapter Four: Caring for Your New Sphynx

The Sphynx cat is a great pet but they are a little more high-maintenance than your average housecat. These cats are very high-energy and they need plenty of daily attention from their owners. If your cat doesn't get the attention and exercise he needs, he may develop problem behaviors or he might become depressed. In this chapter you will learn the basics about cultivating a safe and happy home for your new Sphynx cat. You will also receive some tips about deciding whether to keep your Sphynx as an indoor cat or let him go outside occasionally.

Habitat and Exercise Requirements for Sphynx Cats

The Sphynx cat is not your typical house cat. Many house cats are lazy, preferring to spend their days napping in the sun but the Sphynx is very high-energy and demanding in terms of attention. Your Sphynx will need a lot of daily exercise in the form of active playtime and he will want to spend a lot of time with you as well. If you cannot dedicate a lot of time to spend with your Sphynx cat, it may not be the right breed for you.

In terms of habitat requirements, what your Sphynx cat really needs is space. He needs space to roam around and play – he also needs plenty of toys to play with to help him work off his excess energy. Cats love to climb, so consider buying or building a cat tree for your Sphynx. You can also install shelving on your walls to give your cat a place to perch, watching things from on high. Just be careful about decorating your house with things that can be knocked over – cats are notorious for making a game of knocking things off shelves.

Your Sphynx will not need a crate like a dog does, but you should provide him with a nice comfy bed. Many cat owners find that their cats do not actually sleep in the beds they buy them – they prefer to sleep in boxes or in other strange locations. To encourage your cat to use the bed, try sprinkling it with catnip. You may even want to keep several beds around the house in places your Sphynx is likely to use them – in a quiet room, under a window, etc.

Another habitat factor you need to consider for Sphynx cats is the temperature. These cats do not have a thick coat of fur to keep them warm so the ambient temperature in your house should be a little warmer than what you might consider normal. The Sphynx cat's metabolism works very quickly to help produce enough body heat to keep him warm but keeping your house warm will help to keep his metabolism from becoming overworked. You should also avoid exposing your Sphynx to too much sunlight because his skin is very sensitive.

Toys and Accessories for Sphynx Cats

The Sphynx cat breed is very active and playful so you should keep plenty of toys on hand for him to play with. Each cat is unique in terms of what kind of toys he prefers, so start with an assortment and see what your cat likes. Some of the best toys for cats including small balls, wand toys with dangling objects, small mice with rattles or bells inside, and stuffed animals filled with catnip. You can also make your own cat toys using. Many cat owners find that their cats prefer to play with random objects they find around the house instead of the toys they buy them so don't feel like you have to spend a lot on cat toys.

Indoor vs. Outdoor Cats

When you take your Sphynx to the vet he will likely ask you whether he is an indoor cat or an outdoor cat. Many cats enjoy spending time outdoors because it gives them a chance to roam and they can exercise their hunting skills. There are, however, some potential dangers that come along with letting your cat outside. Not only could he run into predators but he could also be exposed to disease. Outdoor cats need additional vaccinations, so be sure to tell your vet if your Sphynx cat goes outside.

If you consult the experts at the American Veterinary Medical Association (AVMA), they will tell you that it is best to keep cats indoors. While cats do have claws and they can be skilled hunters, they are still fairly domesticated and may not be prepared to survive in the outside world. Cats that live indoors only can reach an old age of 17 years or more while outdoor cats live an average of just 5 years. Not only can being outdoors expose your cat to disease and other hazards, but it also reduces the amount of time you spend with him which could mean that it takes you longer to identify behavioral changes or health problems.

When it comes to the Sphynx cat specifically, this breed is particularly ill-adapted to outdoor life. Sphynx cats do not have a thick coat of fur so they are highly sensitive to sunlight and they cannot regulate their body temperature as efficiently as most cats. Letting your Sphynx cat outside might help him to get some extra exercise, but the potential risks are generally not worth it. You should just spend as much time playing with your Sphynx indoors as you can to meet his needs for exercise and attention.

Chapter Five: Meeting Your Sphynx Cat's Nutritional Needs

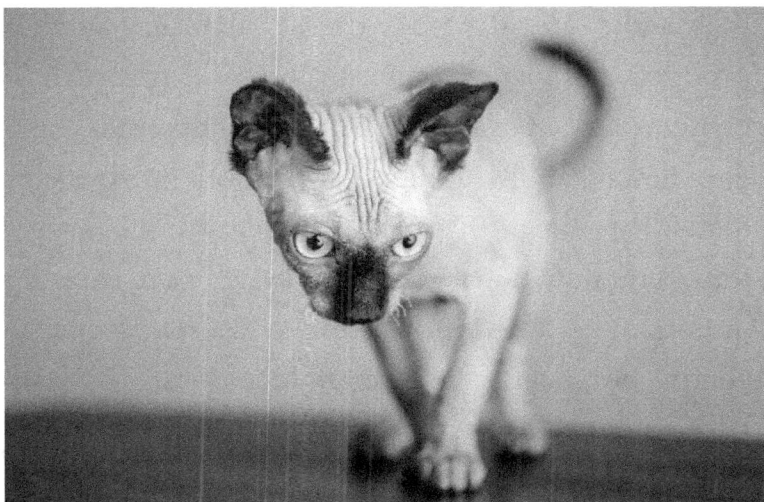

The most important thing you can do for your Sphynx cat's health is to feed him a high-quality and nutritious diet. Cats are obligate carnivores and they have different nutritional needs from dogs, so you need to be careful about which cat food you choose. In this chapter you will receive an overview of the nutritional needs for cats as well as tips for choosing a high-quality commercial cat food product. You will also receive some helpful tips for feeding your Sphynx cat.

The Nutritional Needs of Cats

The first thing you need to know about cat nutrition is that they are obligate carnivores – this simply means that their bodies are adapted to digest and utilize animal products, not plant products. Whereas dogs are mostly carnivorous but can still tolerate carbohydrates, cats have a very limited ability to digest and absorb nutrients from plant foods. This means that protein – meat – is the most important nutritional consideration for cats. Fat is also important because it provides a concentrated source of energy, but meat is the primary focus.

As you may already know, protein is made up of amino acids and it provides the energy your Sphynx cat needs to fuel his healthy growth and development. Protein is important for all cats, but it is particularly important for kittens to help them grow properly. The best proteins for cats come from animal sources like meat, poultry, eggs, and fish. These are complete proteins which means that they contain all of the essential amino acids your cat needs – essential amino acids are simply those that your cat's body is incapable of producing on its own. Plant proteins contain some amino acids, but not all of them

Fat is the second nutritional consideration for cats because it supplies a concentrated source of energy. This is particularly important for Sphynx cats because they need a lot of energy to fuel their metabolism which helps to keep them warm without a coat of fur. Fats also contain essential fatty acids that your cat needs for healthy skin, a strong immune system, and nutrient utilization. Again, fats should come from animal sources like chicken fat, salmon oil, or other fish oils instead of plant sources.

In addition to protein and fat, cats also need and unlimited supply of fresh water and certain vitamins and minerals. Some of the most important vitamins for cats include fat-soluble vitamins like A, E, D, and K as well as water-soluble vitamins like vitamin C and B vitamins. Minerals that are important for cats include calcium, copper, iodine, manganese, magnesium, potassium, selenium, zinc, and phosphorus. Chelated minerals are the best – these are mineral molecules that have been chemically bonded to protein molecules which makes them easier for your cat's body to digest and absorb.

When it comes to carbohydrates, it is important to note that cats have no nutritional requirement for carbohydrates. They are, however, able to digest certain kinds of carbohydrates in small quantities and they can provide dietary fiber as well as certain essential vitamins and minerals. It important to keep your Sphynx cat's carb intake low, however, focusing on protein and fat instead.

How to Select a High-Quality Cat Food Brand

The task of choosing a high-quality cat food can be difficult for some cat owners simply because there are so many different options to choose from. If you walk into your local pet store you will see multiple aisles filled with bags of cat food from different brands and you may also notice that most brands offer a number of different formulas. So how do you choose a healthy at food for your Sphynx cat without spending hours at the pet store?

The best place to start when shopping for cat food is to read the cat food label. Pet food in the United States is loosely regulated by the American Association of Feed Control Officials (AAFCO) and they evaluate commercial pet food products according to their ability to meet the basic nutritional needs of cats in various life stages. If the product meets these basic needs, the label will carry some kind of statement from AAFCO like this:

"[Product Name] is formulated to meet the nutritional levels established by the AAFCO Cat Food nutrient profiles for [Life Stage]."

If the cat food product you are looking at contains this statement you can move on to reading the ingredients list. Cat food labels are organized in descending order by volume. This means that the ingredients at the top of the list are used in higher quantities than the ingredients at the end of the list. This being the case, you want to see high-quality sources of animal protein at the beginning of the list because protein is the most important nutrient for cats. Things like fresh meat, poultry or fish are excellent ingredients but they contain about 80% water. After the product is cooked, the actual volume and protein content of the ingredient will be less. Meat meals (like chicken meal or salmon meal) have already been cooked down so they contain up to 300% more protein by weight than fresh meats.

In addition to high-quality animal proteins, you want to check the ingredients list for healthy fats and a limited amount of digestible carbohydrates. In terms of fat, you want to see at least one animal source such as chicken fat or salmon oil. Plant-based fats like flaxseed and canola oil are not necessarily bad, but they are less biologically valuable for your cat. If they are accompanied by an animal source of fat, it is okay. Just make sure that the fats included in the recipe provide a blend of both omega-3 and omega-6 fatty acids. This will help to preserve the quality and condition of your Sphynx cat's skin.

For cats, digestible carbohydrates include things like brown rice and oatmeal, as long as they have been cooked properly. You can also look for gluten-free and grain-free options like sweet potato and tapioca. It is best to avoid products that are made with corn, wheat, or soy ingredients because they are low in nutritional value and may trigger food allergies in your cat. You also want to avoid commercial cat foods that contain a large amount of carbohydrates since the cat's body is not adapted to digesting plant materials as effectively as animal products. Cats only need a very small amount of fiber.

In addition to checking the ingredients list for beneficial ingredients you should also know that there are certainly things you do NOT want to see listed. Avoid products made with low-quality fillers like corn gluten meal or rice bran – you should also avoid artificial colors, flavors, and preservatives. Some commonly used artificial preservatives are BHA and BHT. In most cases the label will tell you if natural preservatives are used.

When reading the label for commercial cat food products you need to be careful about taking health claims and marketing gimmicks with a grain of salt. Just because the label includes words like "natural" or "holistic", you cannot make assumptions about what those terms actually mean since the definitions are not regulated for pet foods like they are for people food. That is why you are better off checking for the AAFCO statement of nutritional adequacy and looking at the ingredients list instead of just trusting what the manufacturer says about the product.

Tips for Feeding Your Sphynx Cat

Feeding Sphynx cats is a little bit trickier than feeding other cat breeds because you need to find the right balance between feeding your cat enough but not feeding him too much. Sphynx cats are able to get by without hair because their metabolisms produce enough heat to keep their bodies warm. In order to produce that heat, however, these cats need a consistent supply of energy which means access to food all day long. On the other end of the spectrum, however, Sphynx cats have a high risk for obesity so you don't want your cat to eat more than he needs.

Many Sphynx cat owners use an automatic dispenser to ensure that their cat gets as much food as he needs when he needs it. For the most part, Sphynx cats are good at regulating their consumption so that they don't eat more than they need. If you notice that your cat is starting to develop a round belly, however, you might need to start regulating his portions. Some Sphynx cat owners prefer to feed their cats four or five small meals spaced throughout the day instead of giving them unlimited access to food.

One thing you need to be aware of when choosing a cat food for your Sphynx is the fact that they have a fairly delicate digestive system. Canned cat foods are high in moisture and protein which is good for cats, but they can also be very rich. Rather than feeding your Sphynx a diet that consists entirely of canned food, consider purchasing a high-quality dry food and add a spoonful of wet food on top of it just before feeding. You can also try alternating between dry and canned food for each meal.

Another thing you might want to consider for your Sphynx cat is feeding him a raw food diet. The idea of feeding your cat raw meat and bones might sound strange, but it is actually very close to the type of diet wild cats follow – their diets consist almost entirely of whole prey. It is completely natural for cats to eat all parts of their prey including the skin, muscle, organ meats, bones, and connective tissues. If you don't like the idea of preparing raw food for your Sphynx you can easily find fresh or frozen raw cat food online and at certain specialty pet stores. Another option is to choose a dehydrated or freeze-dried raw food that can be rehydrated for feeding.

Dangerous Foods to Avoid

It might be tempting to give in to your cat when he is begging at the table, but certain "people foods" can actually be toxic for your cat. As a general rule, you should never feed your dog anything unless you are 100% sure that it is safe. Below you will find a list of foods that can be toxic to cats and should therefore be avoided:

- Alcohol
- Apple seeds
- Avocado
- Cherry pits
- Chocolate
- Coffee
- Garlic
- Grapes/raisins
- Hops
- Macadamia nuts
- Mold
- Mushrooms
- Mustard seeds
- Onions/leeks
- Peach pits
- Potato leaves/stems
- Rhubarb leaves
- Tea
- Tomato leaves/stems
- Walnuts
- Xylitol
- Yeast dough

If your Sphynx cat eats any of these foods, contact the Pet Poison Control hotline right away at (888) 426 – 4435.

Chapter Six: Training Your Sphynx Cat

While cats typically cannot be trained in the same way that dogs can, there are certain things you can teach your Sphynx cat to do. In addition to training, socialization is also very important for Sphynx cats. In this chapter you will receive an overview of socialization for kittens as well as tips for litter training and dealing with problem behaviors. It is important to have a basic understanding of cat training principles before you bring your kitten home so you can deal with problem behaviors as they develop.

Socializing Your New Kitten

Sphynx kittens are the most impressionable between 8 and 13 weeks of age, though their individual personalities will still be developing for another few months. The Sphynx cat is naturally a friendly and outgoing breed, but you still need to socialize your kitten to ensure that he becomes a well-adjusted adult cat. The experiences your kitten has while he is young will impact the way he is as an adult – if you don't give your Sphynx kitten plenty of new experiences while he is maturing he might respond to new situations as an adult with fear or anxiety.

Fortunately, socialization for Sphynx cats is fairly simple – you just have to give your kitten as many new experiences as you can. Here are some simple suggestions for socializing your kitten:

- Introduce your kitten to friends in the comfort of your own home where your kitten feels safe.

- Take your kitten with you to the pet store or to a friend's house so he experiences new locations (don't introduce him to other cats until he is fully vaccinated, however).

- Expose your kitten to people of different sizes, shapes, gender, and skin color.

- Introduce your kitten to children of different ages – just make sure they know how to handle the kitten safely.

- Take your kitten with you in the car when you run errands – just make sure you have a car carrier to keep him safe.

- Make sure your kitten experiences loud noises such as fireworks, cars backfiring, loud music, thunder, etc.

- Introduce your kitten to various appliances and tools such as blenders, lawn mowers, vacuums, etc.

- Play with your kitten using different kinds of toys and experiment with different kinds of food and treats.

Litter Training for Kittens

For the most part, kittens learn to use the litter box from their mothers so you may not have to do any litter training for your Sphynx cat at all. You will, however, have to make sure that you teach the kitten the location of the litter box and give him some time to get used to it. When you bring your kitten home, take your kitten to the litter box and place him inside. He may scratch around a little bit or he might jump right out – either is fine. Just keep putting your kitten in the litter box a few times a day for the first few days until he gets used to the location. You should also make sure that it is in a quiet, easy to reach location.

If you have more than one Sphynx cat, you should also have more than one litter box. The best rule of thumb to follow is one litter box per cat plus one extra. Some cats do not mind sharing litter boxes but others will refuse to use one that another cat has used. Some cats also use one litter box to urinate and another to defecate. Set up your litter boxes in a quiet, private place that is easy to access. If you have a dog in the house you may need to place the box somewhere he can't get to it – some dogs will eat clumps out of the litter box.

There are many different types of litter boxes to choose from so you have plenty of options. Just be sure that the box you choose is large enough for your cat to get into and move around in easily. In terms of the type of litter, most cats prefer fine-textured litter to coarse litter. You should keep about 2 inches of litter in the box at all times and scoop it frequently and refresh it with new litter. It is usually best to keep less litter in the box and to clean it more often than to use a lot of litter. Just be careful not to choose a litter that is too dusty or one that has too much fragrance added to it – these things could aggravate allergies in your Sphynx cat.

Dealing with Problem Behaviors

Sphynx cats are very smart and very active. While this is usually a good thing, it can sometimes lead to trouble. If your cat doesn't get the exercise or attention he needs, he could become destructive in the house or he might develop other problem behaviors like urinating outside the litter box or scratching the furniture. This cat breed does have some dog-like qualities but you cannot train them to the same degree that you can train a dog. Still, there are some things you can do to help curb problem behaviors.

The Sphynx cat is very smart and he will always be paying attention to you when you spend time together – he will take his cues from you and watch how you react to the things he does. If your Sphynx cat does something you don't like, you should not punish him for it. It is very unlikely that your cat will connect the punishment to the crime and he might just end up being afraid of you. Instead, you need to either teach your cat that bad behaviors don't earn him the attention he wants or you should provide a more suitable outlet for the behavior.

When it comes to things like scratching, you should not try to completely eradicate this behavior. Scratching is a normal and important behavior for cats because it helps them to stretch their toes and to spread their scent through glands in the pads of their feet. If your Sphynx cat is scratching up your furniture, the solution may be as simple as providing him with scratching posts around the house. To encourage your cat to use them instead of your furniture, sprinkle them with dried catnip or use a liquid catnip spray. When your cat uses the scratching post, give him a couple of treats as well to encourage him.

Sometimes Sphynx cats can develop a tendency toward demanding attention – they are also known to become very vocal when they want something. It is important to understand that this is a characteristic of the breed so you may not be able to change it. You can, however, reduce annoying behaviors like incessant meowing by not giving in to your cat. If he meows at you for attention and you give it to him you will only be reinforcing that behavior. If you want your cat to leave you alone while you are working on the computer, for example, just ignore him until he gives up. Eventually your cat will learn when it is play time and when it is not.

Chapter Seven: Grooming Your Sphynx Cat

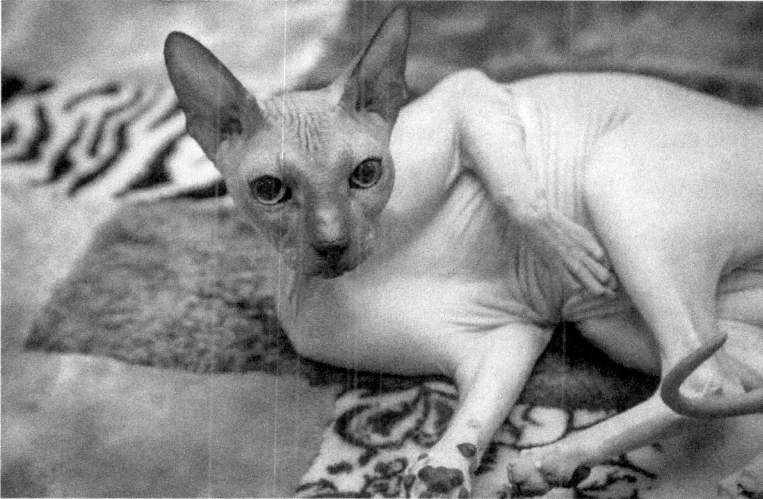

The Sphynx cat has very little fur – just a fine layer of down that might be a little thicker in some places than in others. Because this breed doesn't have as much fur as other breeds it is generally a good choice for allergy sufferers. What many people fail to realize, however, is that Sphynx cats actually require more frequent bathing and grooming than cats with regular coats. In this chapter you will receive an overview of the grooming requirements for Sphynx cats including tips for bathing your cat.

Tips for Bathing and Grooming Sphynx Cats

Because the Sphynx cat doesn't have a thick coat like other cat breeds you might assume that they do not need to be bathed or brushed but you would be wrong. Grooming for cats is not just about keeping the fur clean and free from tangles – it is also about improving and maintaining the condition of the skin. Your Sphynx cat's skin produces natural oils that help to protect his skin and to keep it moisturized. Grooming your cat helps to distribute those oils to keep his skin healthy, shiny, and soft.

To remove accumulated dirt and debris plus extra oil from the skin, you should plan to bathe your Sphynx cat about once every week or two. If you do it regularly, your cat will get used to it and it will not become a major chore. To bathe your Sphynx, fill your tub or a large sink with about 1 inch (2.54 cm) of lukewarm water – you only need enough to get his skin damp. Use a baby shampoo or something that is very mild and fragrance-free and massage it into your cat's skin by hand or using a soft cloth. When you are finished bathing, use a soft cloth and some warm water to remove all traces of soap. Once your cat gets used to the bathing process he may tolerate you pouring water over his back to rinse him.

Other Grooming Tasks

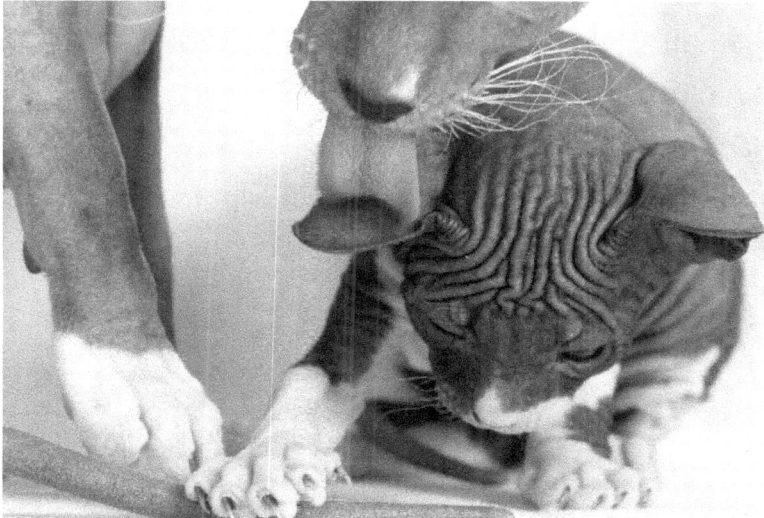

In addition to brushing and bathing your Sphynx cat, you also need to engage in some other grooming tasks including trimming your cat's nails, cleaning his ears, and brushing his teeth. <u>You will find an overview of each of these grooming tasks below</u>:

Trimming Your Cat's Nails

Your cat's nails grow in the same way that your own nails grow so they need to be trimmed occasionally. Most down owners find that trimming their cat's nails once a week or twice a month is sufficient. Before you trim your Sphynx cat's nails for the first time you should have your veterinarian or a professional groomer show you how to do it. A cat's nail contains a quick – the blood vessel that supplies blood to the nail – and if you cut the nail too short you could sever it. A severed quick will cause your cat pain and it will bleed profusely. The best way to avoid cutting your cat's nails too short is to just trim the sharp tip.

Cleaning Your Cat's Ears

Because the Sphynx cat has such large, open ears you do not have to worry as much about ear infections as you might with other breeds. Ear infections are most common in breeds that have folded ears because it limits the amount of air flow to the inner portion of the ear and wet ears are a breeding ground for bacteria. Still, you may need to clean your Sphynx cat's ears occasionally just to remove normal wax buildup. To clean his ears, use a cat ear cleaning solution and squeeze a few drops into the ear canal. Then, massage the base of your cat's ears to distribute the solution then wipe it away using a clean cotton ball.

Brushing Your Cat's Teeth

You will learn more about periodontal disease in Sphynx cats later in this book but for now you should know that keeping your cat's teeth clean is very important. Many cat owners neglect their cat's dental health which is a serious mistake. Brushing your cat's teeth is fairly easy, though you will need a special pet tooth brush and pet toothpaste to do it – you may also need to get your cat accustomed to the toothbrush and the tooth-brushing process slowly. Ideally you should be brushing your cat's teeth every day but if he will only let you do it a few times a week then that is certainly better than nothing.

Chapter Eight: Breeding Your Sphynx Cat

Because the Sphynx cat is such a wonderful breed, you may be thinking about breeding your cat so you can experience the joy of Sphynx kittens. It is important to understand, however, that breeding cats is a major responsibility and not something that should be undertaken lightly. If you do not plan to breed your Sphynx, have him or her altered before 6 months of age. If you do plan to breed, be sure to learn everything you can about the process before you begin – that is what this chapter is here for. You will find an overview of cat breeding information as well as tips for breeding Sphynx cats.

Basic Cat Breeding Information

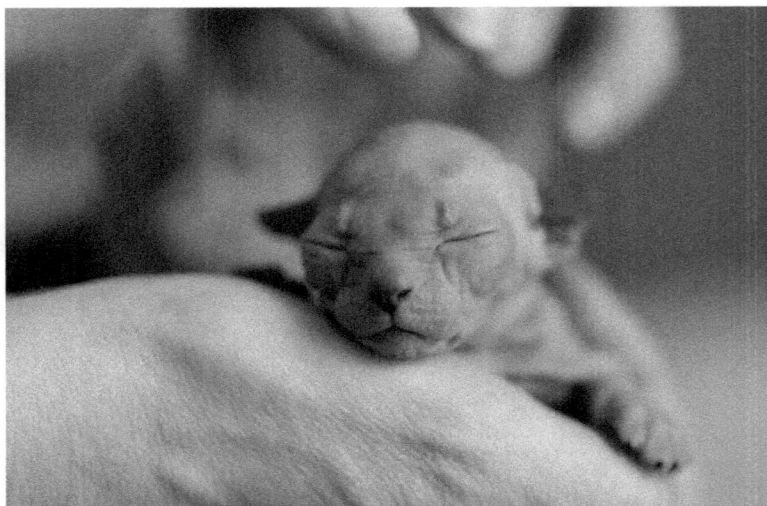

Before you decide to breed your Sphynx cat you need to understand exactly what you will be getting yourself into. Sure, it might be fun to have a litter of kittens to play with but can you spare the time and money to care for them properly? In order to breed Sphynx cats you have to go through a number of steps prior to breeding and then you have to care for a pregnant cat and a litter of kittens. Caring for a pregnant cat and kittens can be costly, so do not breed your cat out of a desire to make money on the kittens – you will be lucky to come out even.

Although the Sphynx cat is a wonderful breed, it is prone to several hereditary conditions including hypertrophic cardiomyopathy and mitral valve dysplasia. This being the case, you need to have your breeding stock DNA tested to make sure that they will not be passing one of these diseases on to their kittens. Also, because the Sphynx is a pedigreed breed, you will need to register your cats with the CFA and register yourself as a cattery if you plan to breed and then sell the kittens. All of these things take time and money to accomplish.

If you are able to jump through the preliminary hoops for registering your cats and your cattery, you can then start thinking about the actual breeding process for Sphynx cats. Female cats in general can go into heat as early as 6 months of age. Heat is another name for the estrus cycle which is the female cat's reproductive cycle during which she becomes receptive to mating. If a female cat in heat is mated to an intact male during her cycle, there is a possibility that she will become pregnant.

The heat cycle in cats typically lasts between 1 and 3 weeks, depending on whether the cat is bred or not. Cats are seasonally polyestrus animals which means that they can have multiple heat cycles throughout the breeding season. In the Northern Hemisphere, most cats cycle between January and September. If you live in a tropical region, your cat could cycle all year round. The actual heat cycle can last as little as 1 day or as long as 7 days. If the cat is not mated, she will go out of heat for a period of 1 to 2 weeks, making the entire estrus cycle last a total of up to 3 weeks.

It is not difficult to tell when a female cat goes into heat. You may not notice any vaginal discharge (one of the first physical signs of heat) but you will notice some behavioral changes. Your Sphynx cat might become even more affectionate than usual, rubbing herself on you or on household objects and rolling on the floor. Sphynx cats can also become quite vocal while they are in heat. Some female cats also urinate more often during heat or they can spray urine as a means of marking their territory.

If you plan to breed your Sphynx cat then you need to know when is the best time to try to get her pregnant. What is unique about cats is that they are "induced ovulators" – this means that the female cat will not actually ovulate until she is mated to a male cat. The act of mating stimulates the release of eggs from the ovaries so, while the cat can technically become pregnant at any time during her cycle, it may take multiple matings within a single 24-hour period for her to actually conceive. Semen can also remain in the cat's reproductive system for several days and a single litter of kittens can have multiple fathers.

Breeding Tips and Raising Kittens

While it is possible for your Sphynx cat to become pregnant during her first heat cycle, most breeders recommend waiting until she is at least 1 year old – many even recommend waiting until she is 18 to 24 months old. The first heat cycle signals that the cat is sexually mature, but she may still be growing and the stress of a pregnancy could impact her development. Male cats usually reach sexual maturity between 8 and 9 months of aged but you should wait until he is about 18 months old to breed him. This will give you time to determine his temperament and to see whether any hereditary conditions manifest.

If you successfully mate your Sphynx cats and the female becomes pregnant, she will enter a gestation period that generally lasts about 63 days. It is important to keep track of when you bred your cat so you can predict her due date and keep an eye on her throughout the pregnancy. You will not be able to tell right away that your cat is pregnant but about two weeks after conception you may start to notice some pinking in the nipple area. After 25 to 30 days you may be able to actually feel the kittens inside her, but be very careful because you don't want to hurt them. X-rays can be used to confirm pregnancy and to count the kittens after about 38 days and ultrasound can be used as early as 14 but it is most accurate after 28 days. The average litter size for Sphynx cats is fairly small, around 4 kittens.

When your Sphynx cat nears the end of the gestation period you should provide her with a nesting box in which to whelp (birth) the kittens. This box should be placed in a quiet, dark area and you should line it with old towels or blankets that you can throw out after the birth. Some of the signs that your cat will give birth soon may include panting or labored breathing, persistent licking of the abdominal area, pelvic contractions, loss of appetite, pacing the room, vocalizations. Once your Sphynx cat begins to give birth, the whole litter should be delivered within 2 to 3 hours. After all the kittens are born, the mother will bite off the umbilical cords and clean them.

It is very important that your Sphynx kittens start to nurse soon after birth because the first milk the mother produces contains essential nutrients and antibodies that will protect the kittens while their own immune systems are developing – this first milk is called colostrum. Sphynx kittens usually weigh between 80 and 100 grams at birth and they are born with their eyes and ears closed. Kittens are completely dependent on their mothers for warmth and food – the mother cat will also lick them to stimulate their breathing and the excretion of waste.

For the first two weeks, your Sphynx kittens will do little but sleep and nurse. Their eyes will open after 8 to 12 days and they will start orienting themselves to sound as well. After 3 weeks the kittens become a little more active, spending more time playing and less time nursing. After four weeks the kittens should start playing with toys and using the litter box – their baby teeth will also start to develop and they may start sampling solid food. A Sphynx kitten's sight is fully developed after 5 to 6 weeks and they will learn grooming skills from their mother after 7.

Between 8 and 13 weeks, your Sphynx kittens will need a lot of socialization. The mother should naturally start weaning them after 6 weeks or so and they should be fully weaned by 8 weeks. During this time, kittens are highly impressionable and you want to expose them to as many new things as possible to ensure that they are properly socialized. By 14 weeks your Sphynx kittens should be weaned, socialized, litter trained, and ready to be separated from their mother and sent to their new homes.

Chapter Nine: Showing Your Sphynx Cat

The Sphynx cat is a recognized breed for both the Cat Fanciers' Association (CFA) and The International Cat Association (TICA) which means that it is eligible for pedigreed show. Showing your cat can be a wonderful but challenging experience and it is also a great opportunity to spend more time with your cat, strengthening your bond. Learning how to show your cat properly can take time, so do not expect to win your first show. The information in this chapter will help to prepare you for showing your cat, telling you what you need to know about the Sphynx breed standard and some general show guidelines.

Sphynx Cat Breed Standard

The Sphynx cat is a beautiful and unique breed that is accepted for show by both the Cat Fanciers' Association (CFA) and The International Cat Association (TICA). The breed standard for each of these organizations is slightly different – you will find an overview of each Sphynx cat breed standard in the following pages.

a.) CFA Breed Standard

General

The most distinguishing feature of the Sphynx breed is the appearance of hairlessness, though it isn't truly hairless. The body is medium-sized with females being slightly smaller than males. The temperament is sweet and lively, the body warm and soft to the touch.

Head and Ears

The head is a modified wedge shape with prominent cheekbones, a whisker break, and a slightly rounded skull. The chin is strong and well-developed, perpendicular in line with the upper lip. The ears are large, broad at the base, open and upright. The eyes are large and lemon-shaped, placed at a slightly upward angle. All eye colors are accepted but should be in harmony with the color of the cat's skin and coat.

Body and Legs

The body is medium in length with a muscular build, rounded chest, and full abdomen. The neck is medium in length, well-muscled, and rounded with a slight arch. The legs are medium in proportion to the body with oval, well-knuckled paws and thick pads. The tail is slender, long, and flexible, tapering to a fine point.

Coat, Skin and Color

The cat appears hairless but has a very fine layer of short hair on the feet, ears, and tail with a peach-like fuzz on the rest of the body. The skin is wrinkled, especially around the ears, muzzle, and shoulders. All colors and patterns are accepted, including white lockets, buttons, and belly spots.

Penalties and Disqualifications

Any hair other than described; delicate or frail appearance; thin abdomen or rump; bowed front legs; appearance of

Devon Rex, Cornish Rex, or Oriental body type; kinked or abnormal tail; aggressive behavior.

Summary of Points:

Below you will find a summary of points to which Sphynx cats are compared in judging. All three categories add up to a total of 100 possible points.

Head (35 points)

- Size/Shape – 5 points
- Ears – 10 points
- Muzzle/Chin – 5 points
- Profile – 5 points
- Cheekbones – 5 points
- Eyes – 5 points

Body (35 points)

- Neck – 5 points
- Chest – 10 points
- Abdomen and Rump – 10 points
- Legs and Feet – 5 points
- Tail – 5 points

Coat/Skin (30 points)

b.) TICA Breed Standard

General

The Sphynx cat appears to be but is not truly hairless. Its skin has the texture of chamois which is very fine and almost imperceptible to the eye and to the touch. The body is warm and the temperament is sweet and lively. The body shouldn't be dainty or small.

Head and Ears

The head is medium-sized with a modified wedge shape and rounded contours. The cheekbones are prominent with a distinct whisker break. The eyes are large and rounded with a lemon shape, slanting to the outer corner. The ears are very large and broad at the base, set upright with a hairless interior. The muzzle and chin are strong and rounded, the profile having a slight to moderate stop. The neck is medium in length, rounded, and well-muscled.

Body and Legs

The torso is medium in size and medium- to medium-long in length. The abdomen is rounded, the chest broad, and the legs proportionate in length to the body. The feet are oval-shaped and medium in size with long, slender toes and thick pads. The tail is whippy, tapering from the body to the tip and proportionate in length to the body.

Coat, Skin and Color

The cat appears to be hairless but may be covered in a short, fine down with or without a puff of hair on the tip of the tail. The whiskers are sparse and short. The hair has a chamois-like texture and the skin is very wrinkled in kittens with adults retaining as much wrinkle as possible. All colors and patterns are acceptable.

Penalties and Disqualifications

Overall small size or thin, frail body; cobby or foreign body shape or composition; lack of wrinkles on the head; non-amenable disposition; any indication of plucking, shaving, or clipping or any means of hair removal or alteration.

Summary of Points:

On the following page you will find a summary of points to which Sphynx cats are compared in judging. All three categories add up to a total of 100 possible points.

Head (40 points)

- Shape – 10 points
- Eyes – 5 points
- Ears – 10 points
- Muzzle/Chin – 5 points
- Profile – 5 points
- Neck – 5 points

Body (30 points)

- Torso – 20 points
- Legs and Feet – 5 points
- Tail – 5 points

Coat/Color/Pattern (30 points)

- Color – 5 points
- Coat – 25 points

Preparing Your Sphynx Cat for Show

Showing your Sphynx cat can be a wonderful experience but it can also be quite challenging. In order to ensure that your cat does well in the show, he needs to be a strong example of the breed standard. Remember, the breed standard for Sphynx cats is slightly different for CFA shows than for TICA shows, so make sure you familiarize yourself with the rules and regulations for the particular show in which you plan to enter your cat.

In addition to making sure that your cat meets the qualifications of the breed standard, there are also some general things you can do to prepare for a cat show. <u>Below you will find a list of general tips and tricks to help prepare</u>

you and your cat for show:

- Make sure your cat is properly pedigreed according to the regulations of the show – you may need to present your cat's papers as proof so be sure to have them ready.

- You have the option of showing your Sphynx cat in the household pets (HHP) category for TICA shows – if you choose this option, be sure to read the unique standard requirements for that category.

- Make sure to fill out the registration form correctly, providing all of the necessary details, and turn it in on time – you may also have to pay an entry fee at this time.

- Clip your Sphynx cat's claws before the show – declawed cats are allowed as well without penalty.
- Make sure that your cat is registered with the organization running the show.

- Be sure to enter your cat in the proper age bracket or category - some organizations allow kittens as young as 3 months.

- Find out what is provided by the show and what you need to bring yourself – some competitions provide an exhibition cage but you will need to bring some things.

In order to make sure that you are fully prepared for the show, pack and bring the following things:

- Your cat's pedigree and registration papers.
- Veterinary records and proof of vaccinations.
- Litter pan and cat litter (if not provided).
- Food, treats, and food/water bowls.
- Cage curtains and clips to hang them.
- A blanket or bed for the cage.
- Any necessary grooming equipment, nail clippers.
- Confirmation slip received at entry.
- Food, water, and extra clothes for yourself.
- Garbage bag for clean-up.

Be prepared to spend all day at the show and bring with you everything you and your cat need to make it through the day. Some shows provide a list of recommended materials to bring so pay close attention to all of the information the show gives you with your registration.

Chapter Ten: Keeping Your Cat Healthy

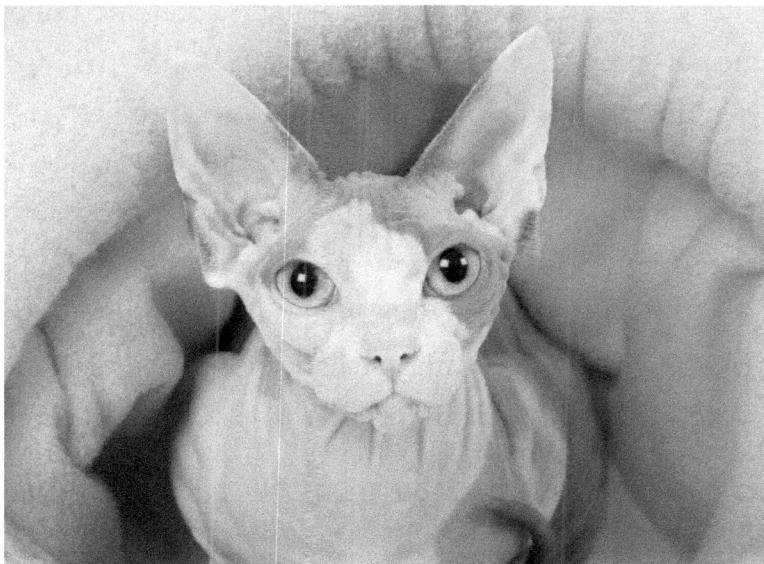

When it comes to being a Sphynx cat owner, your primary job is to provide your cat with all of the love and attention he needs. In terms of the practical aspects of cat ownership, however, you are just as responsible for your cat's physical wellbeing as for his mental and emotional wellbeing. You should take your cat to the vet at least once but ideally twice a year, keep him up to date on vaccinations, and make sure he gets veterinary attention when he needs it. You should also familiarize yourself with some common conditions affecting the breed.

Common Health Problems Affecting Sphynx Cats

Feeding your cat a high-quality diet and making sure he gets routine veterinary care are the top two things you can do to keep him in good health. As careful as you may be, however, you cat can still be exposed to disease. In this section you will receive an overview of some of the conditions most commonly affecting the Sphynx cat breed. By educating yourself about the cause, presentation, and treatment for these common conditions you can help to keep your cat in good health for as long as possible.

Some of the common conditions that may affect Sphynx cats include:

- Cutaneous Mastocytosis
- Hereditary Myopathy
- Hypertrophic Cardiomyopathy
- Mitral Valve Dysplasia
- Periodontal Disease
- Respiratory Infections
- Skin Problems
- Urticaria Pigmentosa

In addition to these health conditions, Sphynx cats are also particularly sensitive to cold and you need to be careful about limiting their exposure to sun since their skin isn't protected by a thick layer of fur.

Cutaneous Mastocytosis

Cutaneous mastocytosis is the name for a disease characterized by the presence of mast cell tumors in cats. Mast cells are formed in the cat's bone marrow but they mature in the peripheral tissues throughout the body, particularly in the skin, digestive tract, and respiratory tract. These cells produce a variety of chemicals which affect the body in different ways in response to certain stimuli. Mast cells can also interact with immune system cells, helping to protect the body against foreign agents.

A mast cell tumor is simply a tumor that originates from the cat's mast cells. These tumors can be either benign (non-spreading) or malignant (spreading and life-threatening). In many cases, the cat develops multiple tumors and while recurrence is possible, metastasis is uncommon in cats. The cause for cutaneous mastocytosis is unknown but research suggest that certain genetic mutations or malformations may play a role. You will be able to identify these tumors as firm nodules or lumps under the skin – some cats also lose weight or exhibit signs of itching with these tumors. Surgery is generally the best form of treatment, though chemotherapy and radiation can work as well. Your vet will be able to identify the type of tumor and recommend a course of treatment.

Hereditary Myopathy

This disease is frequently called Devon Rex myopathy because it is very common in the Devon Rex breed – this breed is closely related to the Sphynx. This condition is generally characterized by muscle weakness due to a defect in nerve signal transmission. Cats with hereditary myopathy may show signs of muscle weakness including tiring easily, reluctance to exercise, muscle tremors, and sudden collapse. These symptoms are most likely to present during periods of stress of over-excitement. The signs of hereditary myopathy can develop as early as 3 weeks of age and they generally progress slowly until the disease stabilizes around 9 months of age.

Hereditary myopathy in cats is an inherited autosomal recessive disorder. Responsible breeding and DNA testing will help to prevent this condition but if a cat carries the gene for the disease from both parents there is nothing you can do to prevent it. If the cat inherits the gene from only one parent, however, he can pass it on but will not show clinical signs himself. Unfortunately, there is no treatment for this condition. When the disease stabilizes in cats the symptoms may taper off. In many cats, however, the disease causes problems with swallowing and there will always be a risk for sudden death by choking.

Hypertrophic Cardiomyopathy

Your Sphynx cat's heart has four chambers – two at the top and two at the bottom. The left ventricle (on the bottom of the heart) is responsible for taking oxygenated blood from the lungs and sending it through the aortic valve (the main artery in the body) to other body parts. For cats with hypertrophic cardiomyopathy (HCM), however, the muscle of the left ventricle becomes thickened and enlarged which may affect its ability to function properly. This condition is very common in cat between 5 and 7 years of age as well as certain breeds. It is generally considered to be the most common form of heart disease in cats.

The cause of hypertrophic cardiomyopathy in cats is unknown in many cases, though there is thought to be a genetic component. Cats with hypertension or hyperthyroidism also seem to have a higher risk for developing HCM. Some of the most common symptoms of this condition include loss of appetite, lethargy, difficulty breathing, weak pulse, abnormal heart rhythm, exercise intolerance, limb paralysis, collapse, and heart failure. Treatment options for HCM depend on the severity of the condition and may include medical treatments to slow the heart rate and to improve blood flow. Keeping your cat on a sodium-restricted diet may also be a part of his long-term treatment plan along with a low-stress environment.

Mitral Valve Dysplasia

Also known as atrioventricular valve dysplasia (AVD), this disease is a condition in which the mitral valve or tricuspid valve of the heart is malformed. For cats with this condition, the valves do not close all the way which means that blood can still flow through the valve when it is not supposed to – it can also result in the obstruction of blood flow due to narrowed valves. These problems can cause the atrium of the heart on the same side of the affected valve to become dilated. Over time, increased volume can raise blood pressure and can even lead to blood buildup in the lungs or in other parts of the body.

Mitral valve dysplasia is unfortunately very common in cats – it may be the most common congenital heart defect in cats. Cats with this condition are also at a high risk for hypertrophic cardiomyopathy, a very common form of heart disease in cats. Some of the symptoms associated with valve malformations include stunted growth, loud breathing, swelling of the abdomen, exercise intolerance, and fainting. Treatment for this condition varies depending on the severity. Some medications like diuretics can help to reduce fluid retention and vasodilators can help to dilate narrowed blood vessels. Some cats also require drugs to regulate their heart rate. Unfortunately, the long-term prognosis for this condition is poor and your cat needs regular check-ups.

Periodontal Disease

If you think that brushing your cat's teeth sounds silly, you may want to rethink your position. Periodontal disease (or gum disease) is incredibly common in cats and it can be very serious. For humans, the most common dental problem is cavities but, for cats, it is gingivitis – a buildup of plaque around or under the gum line. If left untreated, this condition can progress to serious periodontal disease. It could start damaging the tooth or the underlying skeletal structure and bacteria could also leech into the bloodstream, causing a systemic infection.

When it comes to dental disease in cats, there are a number of contributing factors. Normal tartar buildup is simply due to food particles and bacteria accumulating on the surface of the teeth. In some cases, however, dental problems can be secondary to another type of disease or infection. For example, feline leukemia virus and feline immunodeficiency virus can contribute to dental problems in cats like the Sphynx. You will need to have your cat examined by a vet in order to confirm the condition and to decide on the treatment. In some cases it may be necessary to put the cat under general anesthesia for a deep cleaning and to remove any damaged or infected teeth.

Respiratory Infections

Respiratory infections are fairly common in cats, especially if you adopt a cat from a shelter setting. There are various causes for respiratory tract infections but viruses are the most common. Feline herpesvirus and feline calcivirus account for up to 90% of upper respiratory infections in cats and they are very contagious in shelters and in multi-cat households. Some of the symptoms of upper respiratory tract infection in cats including sneezing, coughing, runny nose, congestion, nasal discharge, drooling, fever, loss of appetite, squinting, and depression.

Cats of all breeds and ages can contract respiratory infections but they are most likely to affect cats that live in multi-cat households or that are frequently exposed to other cats. Certain flat-faced breeds like the Persian cat are also more highly susceptible. If you think your Sphynx has a respiratory infection you should take him to the vet for an exam and treatment. Because these infections can be caused by many different things your vet will need to determine the proper course of treatment. Respiratory infections can sometimes take weeks to go away completely so be sure to finish the full course of treatment.

Skin Problems

Because the Sphynx cat doesn't have a thick coat like most cats, their skin is very sensitive. Sphynx cats have a thin layer of fine, down-like hair covering parts of their body but not enough to protect them against cold or direct sunlight. Sphynx cats can actually develop sunburn but it doesn't look the same as it does in humans. In Sphynx cats, sunburn can be a partial thickness burn (similar to first-degree burn) where only the top layer of skin is affected or it can be a deeper partial thickness burn (similar to second-degree burn) where the surface and some of the deeper layers are affected. Deeper burns usually don't develop blisters like they do in humans, but they can still be very painful for the cat.

Not only do you need to be careful about exposing your Sphynx cat to sunlight but you also need to keep his skin clean. All cats produce natural oils from glands in their skin but in normal-coated cats, these oils are distributed throughout the coat by grooming. For Sphynx cats, these oils can accumulate on the skin and cause irritation. This is why you need to bathe your Sphynx cat every one to two weeks. Bathing will also help to wash away dirt, dust, and other particles that can collect on the skin.

Another skin problem that is fairly common in Sphynx cats is related to food allergies. It might sound strange, but most food allergies in pets manifest with skin-related symptoms instead of gastrointestinal issues. If your Sphynx cat suffers from chronic or recurrent skin infections, he could be allergic to something in his food. The best thing to do is to switch to a Limited Ingredient Diet (LID) for about 12 weeks until all signs of the reaction disappear. Then you can either maintain that diet or start introducing potential allergens one at a time until you identify the culprit. Then, all you have to do is pick a diet that is free from that allergen.

Urticaria Pigmentosa

As a nearly hairless breed, the Sphynx cat is prone to a number of skin problems including one called urticarial pigmentosa. This condition is sometimes known as "Devon bumps" because it is also common in the Devon Rex breed. As common as this condition is in the Sphynx and other cat breeds, it is poorly documented and not yet completely understood by veterinarians and other medical professionals. It is, however, thought to be related to nutritional deficiency because it generally responds to fatty acid supplementation.

Urticaria pigmentosa is an inherited condition in Sphynx cats and it usually affects them when they are young. This condition is closely related to allergic phenomenon and certain allergies (to food, environmental pathogens, parasites, etc.) could be the triggering factor for the reaction. This disease typically manifests in the form of tiny red spots which generally appear on the abdomen and neck of affected cats. These spots may be crusted and they often come with hyper-pigmented macula. The most common treatment for this disease is fatty acid supplementation with or without glucocorticoids administered at an anti-inflammatory dose. Some cats also respond well to anti-histamines.

Preventing Illness with Vaccinations

In order to protect your Sphynx cat against dangerous diseases you should speak to your veterinarian about vaccinations. Vaccinations for cats are divided into two categories: core vaccines and non-core vaccines. Core vaccines are those that are recommended for all cats and they include panleukopenia (feline distemper), feline calicivirus, feline herpes virus type I (rhinotracheitis) and rabies. Non-core vaccines are recommended for certain cats depending on certain risk factors such as location and lifestyle. Non-core vaccines may include feline leukemia virus (FeLV) for outdoor cats and Chlamydophila for cats that have been exposed to the virus. Your vet will be able to tell you which vaccines your cat needs.

To give you an idea what kind of vaccinations your kitten will need, consult the vaccination schedule below:

Vaccine	First Vaccination	Booster Shots
Core Vaccines		
Panleukopenia	6 weeks; every 3 weeks after until 16 weeks	1 dose second year then once every 3 years
Rhinotracheitis	6 weeks; every 3 weeks after until 16 weeks	1 dose second year then once every 3 years
Calcivirus	6 weeks; every	1 dose second year

	3 weeks after until 16 weeks	then once every 3 years
Feline Herpes Virus I	6 weeks; every 3 weeks after until 16 weeks	1 dose second year then once every 3 years
Rabies (not in the UK)	single dose, as early as 8 weeks	Annually or every 3 years, depending on type of vaccine
Non-Core Vaccines		
Feline Leukemia	as early as 8 weeks, again 3 -4 weeks later	annual
Chlamydophila	as needed	as needed
Feline Infectious Peritonitis	as needed	as needed
Bordatella	as early as 8 weeks, again 2 -4 weeks later	annual
Giardia	as needed	as needed

** Keep in mind that vaccine requirements may vary from one region to another. Only your vet will be able to tell you which vaccines are most important for the region where you live.

Sphynx Cat Care Sheet

In reading this book you have received a wealth of valuable and practical information about the beautiful Sphynx cat breed and its care. This information will come in handy as you prepare your home for your new kitten and as you get used to life as a cat owner. As you and your Sphynx cat get used to each other you may find that you need to reference certain bits of information from this book. Rather than flipping through the entire book to find what you need, use this care sheet to reference key facts and tidbits about the Sphynx cat breed.

1.) Basic Sphynx Cat Information

Pedigree: result of natural genetic mutation in a domestic cat with a regular coat

Breed Size: normal

Weight: average 6 to 12 pounds

Body Type: medium-boned, well-muscled

Coat Length: very short where present, peach-like fuzz

Skin Texture: wrinkled but soft, similar to chamois

Color: wide variety of colors and patterns

Eyes: eyes are large and lemon-shaped, slanting up at the corners

Ears: very large (2 to 3 inches tall), wide at the base

Tail: long, whip-like; sometimes has a tuft of hair on the tip

Temperament: very friendly and social, lively and active, devoted and loyal

Strangers: makes friends very quickly

Children: very good with children

Other Pets: gets along with dogs and most other pets

Exercise Needs:

Health Conditions: generally healthy but prone to some hereditary conditions; cutaneous mastocytosis, hereditary myopathy, hypertrophic cardiomyopathy, mitral valve dysplasia, periodontal disease, respiratory infection, skin problems, and urticaria pigmentosa.

Lifespan: wide range, average 8 to 14 years

2.) Nutritional Needs

Nutritional Needs: water, protein, carbohydrate, fats, vitamins, minerals

Calorie Needs: varies by age, weight, and activity level

Amount to Feed (kitten): feed freely but consult recommendations on the package

Amount to Feed (adult): consult recommendations on the package; calculated by weight

Feeding Frequency: four to five small meals daily

Important Ingredients: fresh animal protein (chicken, beef, lamb, turkey, eggs), animal fats, digestible carbohydrates (rice, oats, sweet potato)

Important Minerals: calcium, copper, iodine, manganese, magnesium, potassium, selenium, zinc, and phosphorus

Important Vitamins: Vitamin A, Vitamin C, Vitamin B, Vitamin D, Vitamin E, Vitamin K

Look For: AAFCO statement of nutritional adequacy; protein at top of ingredients list; no artificial flavors, dyes, preservatives

3.) Breeding Information

Sexual Maturity (female): average 5 to 6 months

Sexual Maturity (male): 8 to 9 months

Breeding Age (female): 12 months, ideally 18 to 24 months

Breeding Age (male): at least 18 months

Breeding Type: seasonally polyestrous, multiple cycles per year

Ovulation: induced ovulation, stimulated by breeding

Litter Size: about 4 kittens

Pregnancy: average 63 days

Kitten Birth Weight: 80 to 100 grams (0.2 to 0.22 lbs.)

Characteristics at Birth: eyes and ears closed, little to no fur, completely dependent on mother

Eyes/Ears Open: 8 to 12 days

Teeth Grow In: around 3 to 4 weeks

Begin Weaning: around 4 to 6 weeks, kittens are fully weaned by 8 weeks

Socialization: between 8 and 13 weeks, ready to be separated by 14 weeks

Index

D

E

F

G

O

P

Sphynx Cats as Pets

W

References

"About the Sphynx." The Cat Fanciers Association. <http://www.cfa.org/Breeds/BreedsSthruT/Sphynx.aspx>

"Adopting a Second Hand Cat." Kitten Rescue. <http://www.kittenrescue.org/index.php/adoptions/adopting-second-hand-cat/>

"Basic Cat Training." Love That Pet. <https://www.lovethatpet.com/cats/behaviour-and-training/cat-training-tips/>

"Best Diet for Sphynx Cats." Hairless Cat Blog. <http://hairlesscatblog.com/best-diet-for-sphynx-cats>

"Cat Breeding." PetEducation. <http://www.peteducation.com/article.cfm?c=1+2139&aid=891>

"Cat Breeding – Frequently Asked Questions." CFA.org. <http://cfa.org/Breeders/FAQs/BreedingFAQs.aspx>

"Cat-Proof Your Home in 12 Easy Steps." The Humane Society of the United States. <http://www.humanesociety.org/animals/cats/tips/cat_proofing_your_house.html?referrer=https://www.google.com/>

"Dental Disease in Cats." Cat Hospital of Chicago. <http://www.cathospitalofchicago.com/online-cat-health-library/dental-disease-in-cats>

"Estrus Cycle in Cats." VCA Animal Hospitals. <http://www.vcahospitals.com/main/pet-health-information/article/animal-health/estrus-cycles-in-cats/5635>

"Feeding Your Sphynx." Cat Sphynx. <http://catsphynx.com/sphynx-cat-care-and-ownership/food-diet/>

"Glossary of Feline Terms." Cat World. <http://www.cat-world.com.au/glossary>

"Grooming." Kikapoo Sphynx. <http://www.kikapoosphynx.com/grooming.html>

"Grooming Your Sphynx." Joy of Sphynx. <http://www.joyofsphynx.com/2011/08/grooming-your-sphynx/>

"How to Become a Sphynx Cat Breeder." Go Sphynx. <http://www.gosphynx.com/become-breeder>

"Hypertrophic Cardiomyopathy (HCM)." Cornell University College of Veterinary Medicine. <http://www.vet.cornell.edu/hospital/Services/Companion/Cardiology/conditions/HCM.cfm>

"Kitten Development." Australian Sphynx. <http://www.australiansphynx.com/Sphynx_Kittens/Sphynx_Development/sphynx_development.html>

"Litter Box Training for Your Kitten." PetEducation.
<http://www.peteducation.com/article.cfm?c=1+2137&aid
=3288>

"Showing Your Cat in TICA." The International Cat
Association. <http://www.tica.org/showing-cats>

"Should You Have an Indoor Cat or an Outdoor Cat?"
WebMD. <http://pets.webmd.com/cats/features/should-
you-have-an-indoor-cat-or-an-outdoor-cat?page=1>

"Special Nutritional Needs of Cats." PetEducation.com.
<http://www.peteducation.com/article.cfm?c=1+2244&aid
=2575>

"Sphynx." CatTime.com. <http://cattime.com/cat-
breeds/sphynx-cats>

"Sphynx." VetStreet.com. <http://www.vetstreet.com/
cats/sphynx#overview>

"Sphynx Breed Standard." CFA.org. <http://www.cfa.org/
Portals/0/documents/breeds/standards/sphynx.pdf>

"Sphynx Cats." PetMD.
<http://www.petmd.com/cat/breeds/c_ct_sphynx>

"Sphynx – Introduction." TICA.org. <http://www.tica.org/
cat-breeds/item/285>

"Sphynx (SX)." TICA.org. <http://www.tica.org/pdf/
publications/standards/sx.pdf>

"Sphynx Skin Conditions." Sphynx Lair. <http://sphynxlair.com/community/threads/sphynx-skin-conditions.4236/>

"Sunburn on a Hairless Cat." The Nest Pets. <http://pets.thenest.com/sunburn-hairless-cat-10006.html

"Your Cat's Nutritional Needs." National Research Council. <http://dels.nas.edu/resources/static-assets/materials-based-on-reports/booklets/cat_nutrition_final.pdf>

"Your Cat's Nutritional Needs: The Basics." Feline Nutrition Foundation. <http://feline-nutrition.org/nutrition/your-cats-nutritional-needs-the-basics>

"Your Guide to Socializing a Kitten." VetStreet. <http://www.vetstreet.com/our-pet-experts/your-guide-to-socializing-a-kitten?page=2>

Feeding Baby
Cynthia Cherry
978-1941070000

Axolotl
Lolly Brown
978-0989658430

Dysautonomia, POTS
Syndrome
Frederick Earlstein
978-0989658485

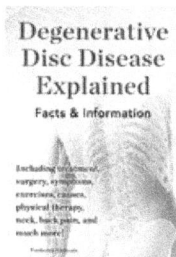

Degenerative Disc
Disease Explained
Frederick Earlstein
978-0989658485

Sinusitis, Hay Fever,
Allergic Rhinitis Explained
Frederick Earlstein
978-1941070024

Wicca
Riley Star
978-1941070130

Zombie Apocalypse
Rex Cutty
978-1941070154

Capybara
Lolly Brown
978-1941070062

Eels As Pets
Lolly Brown
978-1941070167

Scabies and Lice Explained
Frederick Earlstein
978-1941070017

Saltwater Fish As Pets
Lolly Brown
978-0989658461

Torticollis Explained
Frederick Earlstein
978-1941070055

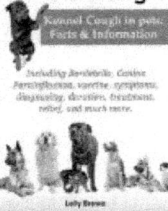

Kennel Cough
Lolly Brown
978-0989658409

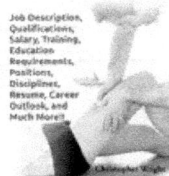

Physiotherapist, Physical
Therapist
Christopher Wright
978-0989658492

Rats, Mice, and Dormice
As Pets
Lolly Brown
978-1941070079

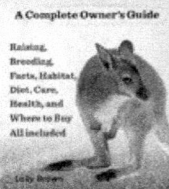

Wallaby and Wallaroo Care
Lolly Brown
978-1941070031

Bodybuilding Supplements
Explained
Jon Shelton
978-1941070239

Demonology
Riley Star
978-19401070314

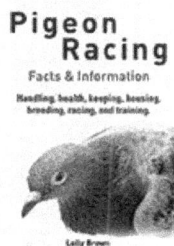

Pigeon Racing
Lolly Brown
978-1941070307

Dwarf Hamster
Lolly Brown
978-1941070390

Cryptozoology
Rex Cutty
978-1941070406

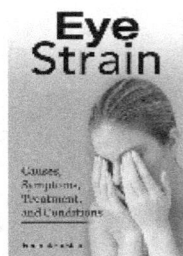

Eye Strain
Frederick Earlstein
978-1941070369

Inez The Miniature Elephant
Asher Ray
978-1941070353

Vampire Apocalypse
Rex Cutty
978-1941070321

www.ingramcontent.com/pod-product-compliance
Lightning Source LLC
LaVergne TN
LVHW051644080426
835511LV00016B/2481